The Gift Of Time

A Story of a Journey through Mental and Physical Agony to Spiritual Health

by Evelyne J. McCollum

LIFEVEST PUBLISHING, INC.

Centennial, Colorado

All Scripture quotations are taken
from the Life Application Study Bible.

The Gift of Time
is written by Evelyne J. McCollum

Published and Printed by:
LifeVest Publishing
4901 E. Dry Creek Rd., #170
Centennial, CO 80122
www.lifevestpublishing.com

Printed in the United States of America

ISBN 10-digit: 1-59879-700-X
ISBN 13-digit: 978-1-59879-700-8

I would love to hear from you. Please send your comments about this book to me in care of the address below. Thank you.
itsok@bellsouth.net

Front cover design by Wally and Trina Gardner
Back cover design by Evelyne McCollum

To: Shirley
with Love,
Evelyne

Table of Contents

Introduction
A Word from the Author

I would like to thank all the people who have been by my side through the journeys spoken of in "The Gift of Time," but they are too numerous to list. God knows who they are, they know who they are and how much I love each of them, so…thank you one and all, my wonderful family and dear friends. Thanks to all of you for your prayers, your concerns, your support, your loving kindness, and you, for just faithfully being here for me. God bless you!

A special thanks to my sister-in-law, Lettie Harrison, for going through my rough draft and making much needed correction of my sentence structure. And to a dear friend, Gayle Moss, who went through my really rough drafts, correcting my punctuation and also improving my word structure. Together they made this a much more readable book. They are experts in their fields and I'm certainly not, so God bless you both for lending me your expertise.

Another special thanks goes to my dear friend, Louise Megargee, for her love and support and for allowing me to use four of her inspirational poems.

And yet another special "thank you" goes to Trina Gardner, a special friend who had given me love and support through everything I have described in this narrative and much, much more. She has also walked the "cancer road" and joins with me in being a survivor. When I was reluctant to begin the journey of book writing, it was Trina's encouragement that gave me the courage to begin and her faith in me that kept me going. She lent her publishing background to improve the quality and content of this enterprise. Without her talent, I would have been lost.

This is a story
of a personal experience
of mine
in dealing with one of life's
greatest challenges.

I call it my
big "C" and bigger "G"
experience.

Chapter 1
The story begins

In the middle of a rather ho-hum night, I awoke feeling thirsty and started down the hall toward the kitchen for a glass of water. I was dressed in a rather sheer nightgown, and as I walked, my right arm brushed against my right breast and instantly, I felt a lump. Think about how amazing that was since I had not felt it earlier that morning when I showered.

I was not alarmed, yet it seemed that God was letting me know that it was something I should see about. I had had regular mammograms for years and wasn't due for the next one for some months, but waiting didn't seem to be an option. So, the next morning I called my primary care physician and made an appointment.

When the doctor examined me and felt the lump, he decided that I should have a mammogram while I was there. As I sat in the dressing room waiting for the test results, I began to pray that nothing out of the ordinary would be found. I had a benign lump removed from my left breast years before and wanted to think even that would not be necessary this time.

After comparing this x-ray with all the previous ones, the doctor called me back in and said that there didn't appear to be anything to be concerned about.

Was this an answer to my prayers?

Unfortunately, not exactly, for the doctor then recommended that I see another physician for what is known as a needle biopsy since there was no denying that the lump was real and felt large.

This next appointment was made for a few days later, and during this time I once again prayed for negative results, and again, the test was negative.

Was this an answer to my prayers?

Again, not exactly, for this time it was decided that I needed a surgical biopsy. The lump, of course, was still there and undeniably, getting bigger.

Had God deserted me?

Certainly it seemed that He had not answered my prayers. But was He simply giving me a lesson to learn and a chance to grow? Maybe. Surely time would tell.

Because my insurance required a second opinion, I would have to see a third doctor before the surgery could be done. I was getting to know a lot of new doctors, it seemed. This doctor was the first to say the big "C" word, Cancer! He suggested that if cancer was found in my right breast, a mirror biopsy should be done on my left breast.

The surgeon, a third new doctor, agreed with the mirror biopsy and he gave me the option of a lumpectomy (surgically remove only the lump) or a mastectomy (remove the entire breast). His opinion was that results were 50-50 as to recovery rates. He told me that he would be comfortable with whatever decision I made.

I began to wonder what would make me feel safe and secure. This was truly a tough decision to make. What would I risk by taking what I considered the easy way out? Talking about being put on the spot, this was it! There didn't seem to be anything to do but pray about it, so I did.

I prayed and prayed but didn't seem to get an answer from God. So, I asked my husband to help me decide, but he felt, and rightly so, that the choice should be mine alone. So, I prayed some more.

No answer yet again! Alas, what to do?

The morning of the surgery came and I still had not decided. But I had run out of wiggle time as I had to tell the surgeon what to do! Both my husband and my primary care physician, a good friend of many years, left the room; neither wanted to influence me in this decision either way. As it was apparent that they would be no help, one more time I asked the Lord what to do, but He seemed to have left with the others. So, with uncertainty if I was doing the right thing, I decided that as long as it seemed to be entirely up to me, I'd rather not be disfigured and opted for the lumpectomy.

As they wheeled me to the operating room, once again I prayed that there would be no cancer and that all of the worry about what to do would have been just "a tempest in a teapot" (a favorite expression of my Irish grandmother). It seemed that I was going to pray until I got the answer that I wanted. I knew I was being a prayer pest, but this was a serious matter.

This was my fifth major surgery and knowing that God had seen me through all the others, I didn't doubt that He would this time, too. The only difference in this surgery was that for the first time, I woke up in the recovery room. It was then I realized that both my breasts were bandaged. Not good news!

Remembering the second doctor's recommendation for the mirror biopsy, I knew that they had found cancer.

The big "C"! Again, I wondered, where was God?

This was certainly not the answer for which I had prayed. It was then that God, in His tender mercy, spoke to my trembling spirit and said, "Yes, you do have cancer, but trust me, it's OK!" Nothing profound, just a simple, "Trust me, it's OK." But God knows my uncomplicated brain and the state it was in at this time, so He spoke in terms that I couldn't help but understand.

Obviously, God was there with me all the time. I was not deserted! Never had been!

It was then I realized this was the lesson I was to learn. What this was teaching me was that Jesus will never forsake us even if, at times, we think He has. I was learning to trust God and not my feelings. We must trust in a God who seems to withdraw at times.

Of course, He was there! But He didn't say "It's OK, you are going to get well"...or..."I'm going to bring you to Heaven to live with me." But think about this, getting well or going to Heaven, what did I have to lose? I was in a win-win situation; to stay with my earthly family that I love so much or to go to Heaven and live forever with my heavenly family.

My heavenly family consisted of all four of my grandparents, my mother who died when I was only two, a few aunts and uncles and last but not least...my father! My father was a wonderful Christian man, who not only taught me to have a passion to live but a security to die. I was with him as he reached out his hand to God peacefully in death. I was so fortunate to have grown up surrounded by such a wonderful group of Christians.

With all these wonderful saints waiting to greet me, I knew that I could not lose!

As Apostle Paul said in Philippians 1: 21, *"For to me, to live is Christ and to die is gain."* God's grace would cover me either way. How great is that!

Looking back, I realize that God woke me to tell me that everything would be "OK" before I was face to face with my earthly family. That is exactly what a loving Father would do, isn't it? He made sure I was prepared so that I could face my family without fear and let them know that they didn't have anything to fear either.

By the way, the lumpectomy turned out to be a wonderful decision, so I guess God did tell me what to do after all! I was probably just trying so hard to hear from Him that I couldn't understand that I already was. I am often still guilty of that.

The next trial I faced was the results from the lymph nodes. My prayer, of course, was that there would be no diseased lymph nodes. Yet, when the surgeon gave us the report, all but one lymph node was involved with cancer. Once again, not the answer I wanted. But God was still there whispering in my ear…"So what? I have already told you to trust me that it's OK."

And then I truly felt deep in my spirit that God was still in control, which left me with nothing at all to fear.

Although now I did not fear the cancer, I felt that there should be things that I could do to fight it. So, I went to a convenient bookstore to search for help in the health section.

After spending a great deal of time poring through the many volumes of cancer-related information, a book caught my eye. The title was, "*Foods That Fight Cancer*." I decided then and there that this was what I was searching for, so I purchased it and took it home to become my new best friend.

I read and re-read this book to teach myself a new diet plan. I found it very easy to live by as it didn't require a drastic change. I found that I basically already ate a fairly healthy diet and I needed only a few minor changes.

"As I was with Moses,
so will I be with you;
I will never leave you
nor forsake you."

Joshua 1:5

Another book I found was "*A Cancer Battle Plan*," which is another great story on cancer and nutrition. If you do research in bookstores vand online, there are many great resources that contain much helpful information.

People have asked me what I thought when I was told that I had such extensive lymph node involvement. The answer is simple.

With God's reassurance that everything was "OK," I didn't find myself trapped by fear, depression or panic. I knew that I was in God's hands and that knowledge calmed any anxiety that I might have had.

I knew that God was taking care of the consequences; my job was simply to trust Him for the outcome. The ultimate victory would be mine with the Lord in control.

So, fortified with a much healthier diet, I was ready for the next development - further tests that were to be done because of the extensive lymph node involvement. And once again, with each test, I would pray that no further cancer would be found.

God certainly heard from me often about this entire situation, didn't He? But, again, the answer came back that there was more bad news; they discovered a suspicious area in my lungs.

Therefore, before any chemotherapy or radiation could begin as originally planned, more surgery would be required. So about three weeks after the first surgery, I found myself in the hands of yet another surgeon. By this time, I thought I had seen enough doctors to last me a lifetime. But, as before, I found comfort in knowing that no matter who the surgeon was, God was in control of the operating room.

During the days in intensive care, I was in and out of consciousness, aware of very little except the presence of God and occasionally, my family. But, I still felt secure and safe when I was alert enough to think about where I was.

When I moved to a regular room, the surgeon and his assistant came in to update me. They explained their long faces by telling me they had removed the lower lobe of my left lung and that the rest of my lungs were completely filled with minute cancers. They then said that this was the worst of all prognoses. In other words, they were giving me a death sentence!

This was shocking news, but not overwhelming. I still had God there holding my hand, so to speak. So I just thanked them and told them I understood. But before I could go back to sleep, they had more bad news. They told me that my lungs looked as though I was a heavy smoker. Yet, believe me, I have never smoked!

I was married to my first husband for at least twenty years before a younger woman took his fancy. He was a three-pack-a-day smoker. This is a good example of what secondhand smoke can do. Not that it caused my cancer…it didn't…but it did make the cancer I had much worse.

This has left me with the firm belief that secondhand smoke should be avoided at all times. I support smoking bans everywhere non-smokers are forced to be with people who, by smoking, seem to uncaringly put not only the non-smokers' health at risk, but foolishly, their own health as well.

My primary care physician, my good friend, was the next person I remember seeing. My dear friend sadly told me that I should spend the next six months as happy and worry-free as possible. This was his way of telling me that was how long they expected me to live. I looked at his sad face and told him not to worry. I said, "Trust me, it's OK." I came to believe everyone decided that I had a very limited vocabulary, for all I ever said was, "Trust me, it's OK."

But then God had said it and I wanted everyone to share in the comfort that it gave me, so I couldn't help repeating it.

Later, my doctor friend told me they really hadn't expected me to live until Christmas, which, at the time, had been only three months away. That is how serious they considered my situation to be.

This dear friend has gone to be with God in his Heavenly home. My plans had been for him to be sitting beside my bedside when I breathed my last. But while that can never be, and I miss him and his caring for me, I am happy to think of him waiting for me to join him in his new home where I'll never need him to "doctor" me again.

We'll both then be completely healed by "The Master Physician"! Praise the Lord!

After the lung surgery, I was told to get as much exercise as my body would allow. During this time, I had a sweet neighbor who was recovering from cancer and needed exercise also. So we decided that we would walk together after dinner each evening.

This was a time that we both enjoyed, not only each other's company, but praying together as we walked. It was a great outlet for both of us. We could share with each other what each of our husbands was unwilling or unable to share with us.

"I eagerly expect and hope that

I will in no way be ashamed,

but will have sufficient courage

so that now as always

Christ will be exalted in my body,

whether by life or death."

Philippians 1:20

"He Himself bore our sins

in His body on the tree,

so that we might die to sins

and live for righteousness;

by His wounds

you have been healed."

1 Peter 2:24

Chapter 2
The story moves on

The diagnosis of metastatic adenocarcinoma of the breast with biopsy-proven metastases to the lungs meant there was one more doctor for me to see, an Oncologist. At this point, I decided that doctors seemed to be ruling my life. Not that it was a bad thing – it just seemed to be overwhelming at times.

The Oncologist told me right away that I would take chemotherapy for the rest of my life, however long that was. He also said that the first six treatments would be especially bad, the old "kill or cure" philosophy, I presumed. I was considered treatable but not curable…
death looming on the horizon.

He gave me a list of the drugs he planned to use and their side effects, so that I would be prepared to handle them. Of all the things that could happen, the hardest thing for me to cope with was the dreaded "hair loss," which every drug listed. Now is that silly or what!

Isn't that petty in the whole scheme of things? What kind of vain person was I? Obsessed with hair - Duh!

My excuse was that, while growing up, my hair had been my shining glory. Strangers would walk up to me and compliment me on my "beautiful hair." Alas, it quickly became my vanity! Would there be a lesson for me in this? You bet! For soon I found that God was ready to wise me up. I was "cruising for a bruising."

Since every drug I was to take listed hair loss as a side effect, I became focused on that alone. I was stupidly forgetting all the other side effects that I didn't focus on; things that were much more serious than hair loss.

So, what did I do? I promptly went wig shopping. Yes, even before that first treatment! After that treatment, the wig went everywhere I did! I guess I thought the least little puff of wind would blow the hair right off my head.

Still obsessed; as you can see, I was ripe for a reality check.

But there came a time when I did focus on all the bad things that could happen to my body. I can't begin to tell you how frightened I was as I prepared to go for that first treatment. I asked my husband to pray with me before we left home so I would feel covered with prayer. After that, I felt more prepared to face whatever the drugs would do to my body.

The Oncologist had already warned me that it would be especially bad and, though it made me anxious, I think he did me a great service in warning me. I did want to be prepared. For me, it is much easier to face the future if I know as much as possible what the future holds.

One morning about four days after that first treatment, the hair-thing happened! Not the wind, but there I was brushing my hair, when suddenly I had more hair in my hands than on my head! Can you believe that I was shocked? I couldn't believe my eyes! Talk about a bad hair day, this was it! The worst hair day of my life and I had had some pretty bad hair days before this!

Well, I cried a few tears, which didn't help, gritted my teeth, which did, put that ever-present wig on and went to work. I probably would have had a big pity party, except for the ladies at work. God bless them, they began telling me how good the "wigged" me looked. But in spite of their comments, I will confess I was too vain to let my husband see me wigless. He missed my "chrome-dome" altogether. In fact, I let no one see me wigless. Oh, foolish me! I was still "cruising for my bruising."

God had a surprise in store to help me overcome my vanity, for one day, my bald head was very much in evidence. I worked at an upscale office park that has a wonderful walking path between the buildings. I still had to walk every day in an effort to rebuild my lungs, so I used that path daily at lunch.

One day as I started out, a co-worker reminded me that it was an awfully windy day. I told her that I didn't mind the wind, without a thought of how I had dreaded the wind blowing the hair off my head. So, bravely, I began my walk completely at ease and as happy as a lark.

Well, I bet you can guess what happened! Yes, there I was walking serenely up a hill toward one of the busiest streets around, at one of the busiest times of day, when a small typhoon hit! My wig blew off my head, filled with air and started rolling like a basketball toward the street.

I began to frantically chase after it. The wig kept playfully staying just out of my reach. Just as I would reach down to pick it up, the wind would gust and blow it another two or three feet away, over and over again. It seemed that the wind was mercilessly teasing me, and with all this comedy in full view of half the city…or so it seemed.

The light was red, traffic was lined up as far as you could see and everyone had an unobstructed and unusually clear view of all the drama unfolding. Well, I did reach the wig just one second before it blew into the street. Then with as much dignity as I could muster, I picked up the wig, shook the grass out of it, put it on and sheepishly smiled at the grinning audience.

I managed to continue my walk with my head up. I was still trying to keep my dignity intact and acting as though that sort of thing happened every day. But, actually there I was, laughing like a crazy woman as I continued my walk.

That was my "cruising for a bruising" hair lesson, learned in the funniest way possible.

I think God has a real sense of humor, don't you? He was probably laughing out loud at all the scrambling around I was doing. Really, this was probably His way of telling me to lighten up; to make me understand that there were many things worse than someone seeing my bald head. At best, it probably made the eyewitnesses' day, giving them a big laugh. I hope so! I know the ladies at work laughed with me as I shared my hundred-yard dash and brilliant fumble recovery.

I was so vain that I refused to allow anyone to see me wigless, even waiting for the light to be out when my husband and I went to bed before taking off my wig. Then making sure I was awake and "wigged" before my husband was awake…really a fanatic about that hair thing.

While all this was going on with me, I had my very best friend, Trina, putting me to shame. Trina, very bravely had breast cancer surgery twice…in essence, a double mastectomy, without the agony of choice I had. She had these surgeries one at a time about one year apart.

She also lost her hair but seemed to be proud of her bald head for everyone got to see it. Trina was then and still is a very beautiful person, which is both an inner and outer beauty; seemingly without any vanity to deal with. Her bald head certainly didn't diminish this beauty at all.

Still holding on to my vanity, I told her that while her bald head was beautiful, mine wasn't. Hers was smooth and perfectly round while mine was lumpy and slightly a bit off center. I told her that sharing my less than beautiful head with others wasn't something I wanted to deal with. No wonder God pulled the "blowing wig" trick on me!

Speaking of sharing…

If you have a loved one with a serious or terminal illness, *please* be open to share your thoughts and concerns and listen to theirs! Don't, for any reason, close them out! It may be very, very hard for you to talk with them about their illness; however, force yourself to do so. They may desperately need to share what they are going through. You can be a great help as you share their pain and remind them of your love as you also remind them that God's love covers all our situations (even hair loss!).

There may be times when they don't feel like sharing and you should respect that as well. Just let them know that you are there for them if the time comes to talk.

At this time, I was married for the second time, as was my husband, and we had been married only about four years. During the weeks of testing after finding cancer and the lung surgery, he was supportive - up to a point. But, he was never available for discussing my cancer or any problems associated with it. He was distant, reserved, remote, and seemingly, unable to express himself. I never knew how he felt. He never told me, for he never once said the word "cancer" or talked about the subject at all.

It was only after my chemotherapy began that I realized one reason he was so "standoffish." He was having an affair with a much younger co-worker; the same circumstances that ended my first marriage. This blow to my self-confidence was worse than cancer. Cancer I could handle, but this…I didn't think I could. The rejection from a second divorce was so much worse than the disease of cancer and created much more stress than I thought I could deal with or handle.

Stress is a danger in a cancer situation, and this was stress magnified a thousand times. I felt that I was the most stressed of any time in all of my life. I had been told to avoid stress at all cost. What was I to do?

After much prayer, my own and those of a few friends in whom I had confided, I decided to confront him with "tough love." Since he was a professing Christian, I insisted that we go to Christian counseling. I loved him very much and wanted to save our marriage at any cost. He reluctantly went to counseling, but refused to take much of a part in the sessions. His heart was already elsewhere.

It was during this time that I actually wore spots on our sewing room carpet, on my knees, praying for my marriage to be healed. We are told in God's word that He hates divorce, so He would have to say yes to my prayers, wouldn't He? He would have to change my husband, or so I thought. The reality of that situation is quite obvious…I was the person God changed!

This was my attempt to interpret God's word to suit my desires. Even in this, God dealt with me with loving gentleness. Through this, I found that prayer is not a way for us to control God. It is simply the way for us to put ourselves under His control, which is a very good thing!

The reality that He taught me was that my husband had a God-given free will and he wanted a divorce. No amount of my prayers could change his heart, for his heart had turned against our marriage. Through this, I learned that God should have always been my focus. Instead, I had foolishly made a "god" of my husband. (Notice the little "g"!) How wrong could I be?

During this agonizing time, I was lying in bed one night unable to sleep, and suddenly, I realized that while my husband was within arm's reach physically, he was hundreds of miles away emotionally. It was then, in my despair, that I decided if this was what the rest of my life would be like…I didn't want to live any longer.

"I hate divorce,
says
the Lord God of Israel,..."

Malachi 2:16

Weakened by chemotherapy and a broken heart, I decided to end it all. I went into the kitchen, poured a bottle of sleeping pills into my hands and stood there thinking how easy it would be. But instead of taking the pills right away, I called my wonderful brother. He convinced me that he loved me, my son loved me and, best of all, God loved me. So what if my husband did not!

I really didn't want to commit the sin of suicide; otherwise I would never have called my brother. But without my brother's love for me and his faith in God, in the midst of my despair, I might have taken the pills. This is an example of how important it is to have a Christian family or Christian friends to turn to for support when you're in great distress.

After talking with my brother long distance for at least two hours, I went back to bed and fell asleep for the short time before getting up to go to work. As I woke up, but still lying in bed, my first thought was: '*If I had taken the pills, the next person I would have seen was Jesus.*' It was as though He looked me in the eye and calmly asked, "Am I not enough?" My heart leapt with joy as my spirit shouted, "Yes, Yes!"

I can tell you, without a doubt, that He was enough then, and He is enough now. He is **the bigger "G"** of this story! God is bigger than we can possibly understand. Truly, I have learned that God is bigger than all my problems or any difficult situation I find myself in. As a matter of fact, He is bigger than all the problems or all the difficult situations in the world, so cheer up…He's got all yours under control, too!

I'm also relieved to discover that I now have no more "little g's" in my life. This has helped me live a more contented life than ever before. By the way, my definition of the rapture is seeing Jesus face-to-face…I can hardly wait.

Neither of my ex-husbands nor their new wives asked me for forgiveness. I believe, in their minds, they thought they had done nothing for which to ask forgiveness. But in order to move on with my life,

God put forgiveness for them in my heart. I wrote both couples and told them I had forgiven them. I received a response from my first husband only, which in itself, was a real surprise. That I heard from no one else was no surprise.

I have found that the truth about forgiveness is that it has a healing sweetness that accrues more to the forgiver than to the forgiven. I also found in the forgiveness there is a small but real moment of liberation all around.

Yet, even after I had allowed forgiveness to rule my life, I still allowed my mind to play all those old "why?" tapes over and over again. I wanted desperately to know where I had failed. Finally, I realized the "why?" didn't matter, and I pushed the erase button, got over it and started looking ahead, not back! I had truly wasted enough of my valuable time in that slimy pit from hell!

Satan had reveled in my misery long enough. It was time I quit allowing him to rule my life with insecurity of who I was and of being filled with anxieties of my worth as a person.

I knew that God loved me. I knew that He thought I was worthy. So what in the world was my problem?

The answer: I was living too much in this world when I allowed "why" to govern my thoughts and not enough in the spiritual world where God was in control and He always knows all the answers to all "whys." Thank Heaven, I finally came to my senses!

"So do not fear,

for I am with you;

do not be dismayed,

for I am your God,

I will strengthen you

and help you,

I will uphold you with

My righteous right hand."

Isaiah 41:10

Chapter 3
So the story continues

After taking chemotherapy for two years, I elected to stop. Wow, was my Oncologist extremely upset with me. He told me that it was his opinion I was committing suicide.

I quote from a memo in my permanent file:

"Evelyne McCollum 12-13-88 8836237

She is now approximately 26 months past diagnosis of etastatic adenocercinoma of the breast with biopsy proven metastatic to her lungs. She is aware, and has been aware for the entire time that we have treated her, that she is extremely lucky to have survived this long and that no one would have expected that her disease would have responded as well to combined modality chemo and hormonal therapy as it has. She is seen today for metastatic re-evaluation. She has had a great deal of emotional stress and she has on several occasions asked me if it would be possible to stop her cancer treatment to relieve her of anxiety, depression, and many psychological symptoms. I believe to do so would be to sign her death warrant. In spite of that, the chemotherapy was discontinued at her insistence in September and she has remained on the Tamoxifen. Major metastatic re-evaluation is accomplished today. She is present for this dictation, more later." William Whaley, M.D

The more later, dated December 22, 1988, was ***"Your present examination shows no evidence of recurrent disease. The chest x-ray reveals surgical changes, nothing to suggest cancer, the mammograms are unchanged since 1986 and do not show any new lumps, and the bone scan was normal. The biochemical profile, likewise, was normal."***

The truth was that while he knew I was terribly unhappy, he didn't know that I had decided long before this that if I made it through two years of chemotherapy, I was not putting my body through any more of the drugs that, while they heal, they also damage as much as they heal.

There had already been a lot of wear and tear on my body, with some side effects that no one mentioned, plus I was just tired of feeling that bad. Anyway, I had already lived a year and a half longer than they predicted, so what was the big deal!

I had been gifted with the sensation that the more I breathed in God's goodness, the more I could feel the Holy Spirit entering my body, defeating all those hateful cancer cells and restoring the damages inflicted by the chemotherapy. It was definitely a God thing!

Then the Oncologist told me that cancer would surely return and that I must accept that fact. I'm sure that he would still tell me that today if I were to see him. But his problem was, he just didn't understand that God was in control, and when I asked Him, God had said, "Go ahead, stop, it's OK." The fact that God didn't mention my cancer cured forever, or facing it again in the future, didn't matter to me at all. Believe me when I say that it still doesn't!

An example of how seldom I think about cancer at all happened several years after this. I was at the Atlanta Symphony one evening and saw the Oncologist's Physician Assistant in the crowd during intermission. She had always given me my treatments and had been very kind and gentle with me. I liked her very much.

Upon seeing me and as she realized who I was, she did a real double take. I'm talking about a true, mouth hanging down to her chest, surprise. Maybe if I said she had a totally stunned look on her face, it would express it better.

At the time, I thought she was surprised to see me at such a cultural event. It wasn't until much later that I realized ....she was surprised to see me at all! You see, she remembered the "death sentence," but I did not! God's "it's OK" freed me from dwelling on cancer. I rarely think of it except to praise God for His mercy and to thank Him for His amazing grace.

And if it does come back, so what...I'm still in a win-win situation!

This story began in September of 1986 and this current year is 2006. That's twenty years! Think about that! Twenty wonderful years with family, friends and a host of wonderful new friends I have met! God is good all the time! All the time - God is good!

Cancer hasn't killed me. Divorce didn't either, although there were times I was sure it would. The Bible tells us that God will use any circumstances for our good if we are called according to His purpose. Knowing I'm called makes me truly believe that God could use both of these terrible circumstances to make me a better person.

It would seem that I was hurt deeply in order that I might be blessed greatly. Believe me, that statement is not as off the wall as it sounds. There have been so many times that I have felt blessed and covered by God's amazing grace as He has moved in my life during this time. I have so many more things than I can describe to be thankful for that this "gift of time" has shown me.

Every day is a great new day to spend worshipping this amazing God we serve. I know for certain that I am closer to God than ever before and pray every day to know Him more and serve Him better. All these experiences created a more vivid thirst to love God more through knowing Him more. This is what I mean by being blessed greatly.

This story is an example of all my prayers not being answered the way I asked because God had a better plan. I would not have chosen to have cancer or to be divorced, but God could see the end of the story, which was a new beginning of trust for me.

God expects us to trust Him to deliver us from harm. He doesn't keep us from adversity…He saves us in the midst of it…maybe by simply taking us to live with Him. How much safer can you get than that?

We should simply ask in humility, having faith that God has already prepared the best answer. God knows exactly what we need to shape and mold our lives so that we become an offering of praise to glorify Him, and that's as it should be.

The doctors might tell you that I'm living on "borrowed time," as they told me. But I know it is a gift. God's gift of time! God is still in control and He is the schedule maker. We live and die in His time and since I'm living on "divine time"; it just isn't my time yet!

"Do not be anxious about anything

but in everything,

by prayer and petition

with thanksgiving present

your request to God.

And the peace of God,

which transcends all understanding,

will guard your hearts and minds

in Christ Jesus."

Philippians 4:6 & 7

Chapter 4
And the story still goes on…

In the beginning of this adventure, I made an early decision not to tell anyone other than my husband that the doctors had given me only six months to live. I didn't want anyone to fix a date in their minds to remind them that I had only so many days left.

I certainly had no fixed date in my mind. I was content to live each day, one day at a time, and enjoy it to the fullest of my ability. I didn't feel that God had put an expiration date on my time card and I trusted totally in God's Time Table.

Since I was not anxious about time, I didn't want those who loved me to be anxious either. While this worked for me, I realize this approach is not for everyone. Each person must decide what is best for them and for their loved ones.

There were so many wonderful Christians who were instrumental in my recovery process. There are far too many to name here but I will mention a few.

From the beginning of knowing I had cancer, along with my family, I asked many Christian friends for their prayers. I had letters from churches, near and far, wishing me well and telling me of their prayers. These prayers for me acted as an anchor in my sea of emotional distress. What great comfort it was to be lifted up in prayers by so many believers.

Another example of God at work in my life and speeding up my recovery was Metro Bible Study. I attended this Bible study every Tuesday night for years and was blessed every time I was there.

This Bible study was started by a wonderful Smyrna couple in their basement with a few teenagers. It was so blessed that it soon outgrew the basement and moved to a small local church. That was soon outgrown, too, and it was moved to a larger church. Attendance kept growing and once again it became necessary to move to a much larger church.

God was truly blessing this study as there were many hundreds of Christians, both young and older, that attended regularly. John Riley, the teacher of the study, was a wonderful Christian speaker and attracted all age groups from all walks of life. He inspired all of us with his God-given ability to bring the gospel to life.

The lady who began this study was a very devout Christian named Jackie Ellis. Jackie and her husband, Charles, became known to everyone as Mom and Pop Ellis. To everyone, these two wonderful people became family.

Jackie became one of my dearest friends and the one person that I turned to most often for spiritual advice. I never called her that she didn't have some godly advice for me or she would tell me where to find the answer to my question in the Bible.

She was a very wise, a very kind and a truly loving person. She was there for me through all my surgeries and treatments. She even held my hand through my divorce agony, praying for me daily. Truly she blessed my life in so many ways.

Jackie was stricken with colon cancer about a year after my cancer was diagnosed. As painful and debilitating as her cancer was, she did not let it interfere with her role in Metro. She never complained about her illness at all.

When she needed help, I tried to be as strong for Jackie as she was for me. I felt so blessed to be of service to her in any way that was available to me. One evening I was staying with Jackie while Charles was feeding the homeless in downtown Atlanta, which was something the Bible Study did every Friday. During this time Jackie became so ill that I had to rush her to an emergency room.

But the next Tuesday night, she was at the Bible Study as though nothing was wrong. She was a truly amazing example of faithfully accepting whatever God had planned for her without complaint.

God decided to take Jackie home to live with Him, which left a great void in many lives, including mine. At the celebration of her going home, there were thousands of people there. Each one was there celebrating having been blessed to have been "touched by an angel."

Jackie's death caused me great confusion. I couldn't understand why God would take such a wonderful leader who had been such an inspiration to thousands and leave me here. I even went through a period of time where I felt almost guilty to be the one spared.

God finally let me know that when He takes a life and spares a life, it is for His glory and our good. He let me know that Heaven needed Jackie, too. It just took me a while to realize this and to remember that Jackie was exactly where she should be and now had a new healthy, cancer-free body.

In my anxiety to recover from the agony of being divorced, I even attended several divorce recovery programs such as Fresh Start, which I attended twice. I later found a divorce recovery program at a local church that was meant for one eight-week period of sessions, which I stretched into two. As I have said, I was determined to recover from this agonizing thing called divorce, no matter how long it took or how many seminars I had to attend.

At last, after three long years, I became determined that divorce was not going to rule my life forever. Three years! What a waste of my "gift of time"!

Through a friend, I also found a wonderful ladies' prayer group that met every third Saturday night. What wonderful support those dear Christian ladies were, even though they were in as much pain as I was. Yet each of these sweet ladies offered their support to each of the other ladies that were attending. Each week we held each other up with prayer. I'll forever treasure their loving kindness with a full and grateful heart.

A Christian co-worker of my husband sent me word that his little four-year old son asked God to bless me every night. Can you imagine how that touched my heart!

Neither the child nor his father knew me personally, but showered me with God's love by lifting me up in their prayers.

It still blows me away just thinking about it! I especially treasure that child walking in God's love at such a young and tender age.

God has always gifted me with a positive attitude and with all these dear Christians praying for me, I found my already positive attitude growing by leaps and bounds. Once again, I could visualize the Holy Spirit circulating through my body, destroying all those diseased cells with every breath of God's healing energy that I took.

And doctors will tell you, some doctors anyway, that a positive mental attitude cures more ills than their medicine ever does! My dear doctor friend had me share my cancer experiences with another doctor whose diagnosis was the same as mine. My friend asked me to tell the other doctor if I thought that their medicine cured me, or if it was truly God.

How about that for the medical profession! My friend gave me the opportunity to give God the glory for what had happened during my illness. Of course, my answer was, "I truly believe that God used the medical skills He gifted you with to cure me as an example of His power."

Isn't it wonderful that we can trust God to take care of all our consequences, not only cancer but everything that happens in our lives? Our responsibility is to simply trust in whatever means He uses to accomplish His will for us. If we trust Him faithfully, the victory of all consequences is ours in the Lord.

As we deal with cancer, we must remember that there are things that cancer can't do. Cancer can't kill faith in a Sovereign God who loved us enough to die for us.

Cancer can't keep us from enjoying each and every day that is allotted us. All it takes is for us to remove our focus from cancer and just look around at the beauty of God's love that shines through every dark cloud of pain and despair.

"Our destiny is home with our Father in Heaven. It is so easy on this journey to lose sight of our destination and to focus on the detours of this life instead. This life is only the trip to get home. One hour of eternity, one moment with the Lord, will make us utterly forget a lifetime of darkness." Bob Snyder

I truly believe with Mr. Snyder, that this life is truly only the journey to eventually be welcomed to our Heavenly Home and spend an eternity there that is filled with endless love.

I would like to share one of my favorite scriptures with you which says...

"I have said this to you so that in Me you may have peace. In this world you have tribulations; but be of good cheer, I have overcome the world."

John 16:33

It comforts me just to think that no matter what happens or how ugly it is, God is still in control! He's still bigger than whatever comes our way. Always was, always will be!

As I close, I ask you to realize this...There are three orders of affliction:

- One, that which comes simply because we share in the fallen nature of the human race.
- Two, those which (by God's permission) come from the malice of Satan trying to bring us back under bondage. Satan hates for us to be free.
- Third, those directly from God Himself to purify and refine us.

The three orders of affliction sometime seem to overlap, but wherever they come from, God can and does use them to accomplish His work in us. Amazing, isn't it?

As you read this account, please take with you a heart's desire to minister to this messed up and wicked world that we live in. God doesn't really need us to complete His work. As a Sovereign God, He is quite capable of doing that Himself. We're just so very blessed that He chooses to use us. But the effectiveness of our actions is in direct proportion to the dedication we have behind them. The result of our offering must be left up to Christ. Our duty is obedience. The outcome is up to God!

I have often wondered why God has spared me, turning this bad time in my life to good. Maybe it was simply for me to write this account to remind you that this great and awesome God we serve is a Sovereign God in control of the universe...the bad as well as the good.

With the knowledge that God is in complete control, we can relax and let Him take charge of all our ups and downs. What a relief to relinquish control to an Almighty God whose wisdom is beyond our ability to comprehend!

God's "Trust me, it's OK" has given me a contentment that passes all understanding. I now live every day as contented as it is possible to be. Yes, even during the storms that come my way!

There is both beauty and pain in this wicked world we live in. All we have to remember is that God is faithful to walk with us through each and every day. Let's begin to forget the baggage that we carried around for years, the problems that don't matter any more, the tears that we have shed and fix our eyes on the beauty of God's creation.

All you have to do is put your complete faith in a loving Savior who loved you enough to die for your sins and you can have this peace that passes all understanding, too!

So, let's simply put our hand in His and say, "Thank You, Lord for loving me and setting me free. It's OK, God, everything is great! So, come on Lord, I'm ready to celebrate!" Then in victory, the Heavenly Host will join us, dancing and singing with joy!

It's true, I have reached a stage of contentment with my lot in life that is beyond belief. But it has still left me with a thirst for more knowledge of this awesome God we serve. It seems that the more I know, the more I want to know, and that, too, is as it should be.

Oh, by the way, can you guess what my e-mail address is? It has become my life's slogan…(itsok@bellsouth.net)

Let me leave you with this thought: God is most glorified in us when we are most satisfied in Him. So, let's resolve to live a fully satisfied life, worshipping our Sovereign God, who with only love in His heart, died to save us.

"We know the love

that God has for us,

and

we trust that love."

1 John 4:16

"And this is love;

that we walk

in obedience to

His commands."

2 John 1:6

Chapter 5
The Gift of Time
(October, 1986)

With long faces six months the doctors said.
But then God spoke and said, *"No, I have other plans."*
You're on 'borrowed time' was their reply.
"Not true," God answered back. *"It isn't 'borrowed' at all.*
It is my gift of time."
My prayer is that I find wisdom to use
this gift for the purpose it was intended.
May I walk the path God chooses, greeting those I meet
and recognizing their needs,
then act accordingly.
Making every day count for all it should.
I pray that no time is wasted in looking back
at what-ifs or why-me(s).
Life, at best, is too short for such thoughts.
There is joy every day that God loves me,
and in knowing that when He decides,
I will be with Him for eternity,
the real "gift of time."

Written 2006

"For God so loved the world that

He gave His one and only Son,

that whoever believes in Him

shall not perish

but have eternal life."

John 3:16

May God bless you daily, is my prayer!

This poem was first written in May of 1990 and, at that time, I had lived forty-three months longer than the doctors had given me, plus endured two long years of chemotherapy. As I have said, after the two years I elected to stop the chemotherapy, which gave the doctors concern as they said this was certainly a death sentence I was imposing on myself.

But here I am, still blessed by God's earthly gift of time and forever ready for His Heavenly gift of joy. Just as Peter Pan's "ticking crocodile" was always chasing after him, so is "old man time" always chasing after each of us.

This makes me realize every day how very thankful I truly am for my added time with those I have always loved, and how grateful I am for each new person that He has placed in my life. I am truly blessed by it all.

Some thoughts about "Time" or "Time and Beyond Time":

Our life comes to us moment by moment. One moment disappears before the next comes along; and there is room for very little in each. That is what "Time" is like. And of course, you and I tend to take it for granted that this "Time" series...this arrangement of past, present and future...is not simply the way life comes to us, but the way all things really exist. We tend to assume that the whole universe and God Himself are always moving on from past to future just as we do.

But almost certainly God is not in "Time." His life does not consist of moments following one another. Every moment from the beginning of the world...is always the "Present" to Him.

If you picture "Time" as a straight line along which we have to travel, then you must picture God as the whole page on which the line is drawn. We come to the parts of the line one by one; we have to leave A behind before we get to B, and cannot reach C until we leave B behind. God, from above or outside or all around, contains the whole line, and sees it all.

But suppose God is outside and above the "Time-line." In that case, what we call "tomorrow" is visible to Him in just the same way as what we call "today." All the days are "Now" for Him.
(Quoted from C.S. Lewis' "Mere Christianity")

I am very happy to think of "My Gift of Time" in this "Now Time" as though I am living in the "Beyond Time" with God.

A thought: Remember, always look with gratitude, not at the gifts, but at the Gift Giver…God. Time itself, and all that time means to us, is given to us by God.

"Every good gift and every perfect gift is from above, and cometh down from the Father of lights."

James 1:17

Now there is only one thing to decide and that is as Gandalf told Frodo in the Friendship of the Rings: "All we have to do is: decide what to do with the time that is given us." What I have decided to do is: wake up each morning and say:

"This is the day the Lord has made…
I will rejoice and be glad in it…"

Psalm 118:24

"But do not forget this one thing,

dear friends;

with the Lord a day is like

a thousand years,

and a thousand years

is like a day.

The Lord is not slow

in keeping His word."

2 Peter 3:8

Today

Each morning I wake to find God has given me
a new day, a beautiful gift to use.
I can spend it in my own way; He lets me choose.
I can let a gloomy morning make me sad,
or see God's plan for it and be glad.
I can waste my day waiting for tomorrow;
trading possible overwhelming joy
to take a chance on futile, useless sorrow.
The sad fact is when tomorrow comes
today is no more.
It is gone forever, even God does not restore.
So, my prayer is that my today be not loss but gain;
giving everyone joy and no one pain.
That at the day's end no one has been hurt by anything I've said or done.
I pray this day was a blessing to all, another victory won.
I fervently pray that God is pleased
as I lay down to rest.
That my day has given Him honor and
His name has been blessed.
For truly, if He chooses to give me another day, I promise to spend
it rejoicing in exactly the same way.

Evelyne McCollum

Always remember this:
"In the arms of God, there is no time.
There is only love.
That's what we call eternity, not endless time,
but endless love.
If you have love, you have all the time
in the world…right now!"

John Robert McFarland

"Give Thanks to the Lord,
for He is good;
His Love endures forever."

Psalm 106:1 & 107:1

I am so blessed that God's "It's OK" has given me a hope and joy that is independent of outward circumstances. This hope and joy, which is the deepest form of happiness, comes only from following Jesus, no matter what the cost.

The end of the beginning

And life goes on!

Chapter 6
A New Beginning
(And it is still OK!)

With what started as a routine chest x-ray that showed a small abnormality in my right lung in August of 2006, I began my next journey with the Big "C" (that dreaded cancer word). That small abnormality began a series of tests; I think every test known to mankind. These results of these tests developed into a determination that there was a recurrence of cancer in my right breast.

So far, tests have shown an almost absolutely clean bill of health as far as the lung is concerned. It's amazing how God works, isn't it? A routine chest x-ray that alerted doctors to test my lungs found breast cancer!

I'll never understand how God works all things out, but that's OK, I'm just proud that I'm included in His plans!

That August, I began to see some new doctors. I felt that I should tell every doctor that I was seeing that no matter what they found, I would not expose my body to any more chemotherapy. Two years of my system being invaded by all those poisons seems to me to be enough for any lifetime.

But I did not make this decision without praying about it. I felt once again that God was saying that it was "OK" with Him to skip chemotherapy. He seemed as near as He had in the past. So I had no doubt that this was the right decision for me.

Not a single doctor challenged me on this as long as I approached my decision from a completely informed medical evaluation…so, all the tests were ordered. Regardless of test results, I knew my decision would remain the same and it will continue to be the same.

God's approval was all that I needed to feel comfortable, regardless of test results. But, as I did before, I prayed before each test that there would be no cancer.

Again, God answered my prayers His way, which again, was not how I prayed. But I knew, as before, I should accept this as God's will, for it must be the best for me.

Thus I began my adventure with new doctors. I am very impressed with the lung specialist who is associated with the Georgia Lung Association. He and his group have been most professional while being very compassionate.

This new Oncologist is with the same group as my previous Oncologist. When I mentioned this to my new doctor, he told me that I could still use the first doctor if I chose to do so, which I didn't.

The original treatments were done in Atlanta and the new Oncologist is located very near to where I live in Smyrna. Why drive that distance when I don't have to?

The original Oncologist was a great doctor, but not a very compassionate man. My new Oncologist is also a great doctor and very tender-hearted. I consider that a plus in my favor.

I have had the opportunity to tell the Lung Specialist, the Oncologist and the Radiologist that I think they are God's gift to me and that He has given them the tools to minister to me as He directs their actions.

The current diagnosis is: Metastatic Breast Cancer, which is ER1PR positive. The treatments that I will undergo are radiation and an oral medication - Femara. Radiation will be in the right breast area and zapping the lymph nodes in that armpit.

Treatments will be five days a week for a minimum of six weeks. Having treatments this often, which is standard I'm told, will curtail some things that I have planned, but that's a small blip in the scheme of things. I can deal with that without a problem.

As I have said, along with the radiation treatments, I will be taking Femara, which is an upgraded form of the drug, Tamoxifen, which I had taken with my first occurrence of cancer.

Both drugs are Estrogen blockers prescribed because all my cancer has been Estrogen dependent. I took Tamoxifen during my chemotherapy and for about five years after I elected to quit that treatment. I had very little side effects from the Tamoxifen and as this Oncologist has told me, the most general complaint with Femara is severe "hot flashes."

I can deal with "hot flashes," but if it gets to be a problem and they are too severe, the Oncologist says he can help remedy that. How long I'll take this drug has not been discussed and I suppose it does not really matter. I'm sure the doctor will know when enough is enough, or God will let me know when it is "OK to stop."

At some point in time, if all this fails to curb the cancer, I will need to consider surgery. I am praying and asking my family and friends to pray for NO SURGERY! But as always, I bow my will to the will of God.

His "It's OK" from the very first time I realized that I had cancer back in 1986, is still resounding in my mind. I still believe with all my heart that whatever God has in store will be the best for me, even surgery.

At every step through this new journey, doctors and nurses have asked me about my anxiety level. Please know as I have told each of them…I have no anxiety!

My first lung specialist, after he had given me the six-months death sentence, asked me once about my anxiety. He said, "I know you seem to be this serene swan calmly swimming around, but tell me, aren't you just paddling like a bat out of hell under the surface?" My answer to him was, "What you see is exactly who and what I am. I'm just as calm below as I am on the surface."

If I had no anxiety then, how could I now? This is a walk in the park compared to the death-knell from before.

I have asked that my family and friends share in the peace I have with all this. The only thing that would disturb my peace of mind would be worrying about their peace of mind. I asked them to think on this …I've had twenty wonderful years to enjoy being with them.

I have been privileged to see my "almost grandchildren" grow up to be two very special Christians and truly wonderful young people. They are my brother's grandchildren, but as I have none, he has been generous to share his with me.

I have always said that if my cancer came back, it would be "OK" and it is! I pray to glorify God as I walk on this journey, and as before, I have prayer partners that will walk every step with me. The comfort of all these prayers will make this journey an easy one, just as the prayers of the past made that journey easy.

I count it all joy that I have been blessed to share my life with the two best Christmas presents known to man…my son and His Son, how great is that!

What a "gift of time" I've had! And I'm still enjoying my "gift," which the new Oncologist insists, though he confesses he is not God, will be twenty more wonderful years. What a thought!

(I guess that, as of yet, I still haven't been stamped with an expiration date!)

Because of my "gift of time," I have learned that life is not measured by the number of our breaths…but by the moments that take our breath away! God has given me many special moments that have taken my breath away.

Moments that only God knows how wonderfully special they are. Simple moments, yet very joyous moments of time, in which He has proven His love for me over and over again.

Beautiful sunrises, glorious sunsets, the laughter of children at play, friendly smiles on beautiful faces, voices lifted in melodious song, an "I love you" from family and friends, a hug just when you need it… simply an endless treasure of "butterfly moments" to hold in my heart.

Moments to remember that have pierced me with God's amazing goodness. Each time, it's as though He smiles on me and says these are just for you…all just for you. What an awesome, loving God He is and what humbling experiences these moments are!

"Finally, brothers, whatever is true,

Whatever is noble, whatever is right,

Whatever is pure, whatever is lovely,

whatever is admirable…

if anything is excellent or praiseworthy…

think on these things.

Whatever you have learned or received

or heard from me, or seen in me…

put it into practice.

And the God of peace will be with you."

Philippians 4:8 & 9

"Something strange happened, for that one moment you had the feeling that God and you were one. By the Grace of God it has been given you to see the infinite beauty of the world which is only the reflection seen through a glass darkly of the beauty of God. The essence of joy, that vision of His beauty will remain with you till the day of your death."

The Razor's Edge by Somerset Maugham

I call my special moments "butterfly moments" because like the beautiful butterfly that lives such a brief time, so do most of our beautiful moments. But the memory of those moments will remain with us to hold in our hearts forever.

I have always been fascinated with the awesome metamorphosis of an ugly caterpillar to become the beautiful butterfly and compare it to our even more awesome metamorphosis from sinners to saints. Both are acts of God to complete His plan for us. I think of this metamorphosis as my "butterfly experience." It's truly a God-thing!

The amazing grace of this simply takes my breath away!

While I saw myself as a lowly caterpillar trapped in my cocoon of despair, rejection, sin and self-pity, God had always seen the butterfly He meant me to be. As I realized this, He gently lifted me out of my earthbound cocoon to soar on gossamer wings of glistening joy...... becoming a beautiful new creature, reborn, through His grace.

A gift born of God's great love through His Son, that was unearned, unconditional, eternal and absolutely free.

Awesome isn't it? Absolutely blows my mind!

"What use the glad wings of a butterfly, if it is earthbound with thoughts of its contemptible past?"

Author unknown

For those of us that take this troublesome journey on such a rough and rocky road we call cancer, I would ask everyone to pause and remember this:

WHAT CANCER CANNOT DO

Cancer is so limited…
It cannot cripple
Love
It cannot shatter
Hope
It cannot corrode
Faith
It cannot destroy
Peace
It cannot kill
Friendship
It cannot suppress
Memories
It cannot silence
Courage
It cannot invade the
Soul
It cannot steal
Eternal Life
It cannot conquer the
Spirit.

Author Unknown

"I praise You because,

I am fearfully and wonderfully

made;

Your works are wonderful

I know that full well."

Psalm 139:14

I have learned that death is not only invincible but a joy to look forward to. Truly in the midst of every sorrow there is a hidden joy… there is a spiritual aspect that God is still in control, and only He can walk us safely through the "Valley of the Shadow of Death." We need to always remember that death is not our ultimate enemy and keep in mind that its "final word" is our gateway to heaven.

Although I don't think it will, cancer could win this battle. But if you hear that it has, don't give it another thought, for God and I will have won the war. I will still have all those things mentioned previously that cancer can't steal from me.

As I have said before, I'm truly in a "win-win" situation… here or Heaven? It just does not get any better than that. So, if you hear of my death; keep this thought in mind and celebrate with me!

Celebrate With Me!

If my parting has left a void,
Don't be burdened with thoughts of sorrow.
Remember that I've merely gone home
to enjoy the sunshine of each tomorrow.
Celebrate with me!

I have spent my "gift of time"
to laugh, to love, to work and play.
There is peace that things left unsaid or undone
must now stay that way.
Celebrate with me!

Remember my life has been filled
with many good times and, yes, some sad.
But filled with God's mercy,
the good far outweighed the bad.
Celebrate with me!

I've walked the path that He planned for me
since I took His hand when first I heard His call.
Now, He's called me home. He's set me free!
Lift up your hearts, one and all.
Celebrate with me!

Take joy in knowing I'll be waiting
when your "gift of life" runs out.
Then we'll spend eternity together.
For that's what God's love is all about!
Celebrate with me!

Evelyne McCollum

Chapter 7
Good News!

In January 2007, I had good news! Both the Radiologist and the Oncologist told me that my tumor has vanished and my lymph nodes seem to be back to normal with the current radiation treatments and continued oral medication.

When I had my final radiation treatment at the end of February, the Radiologist checked me out, asked me to come back later for a final inspection of my skin condition, then smilingly said that they would miss me.

Guess what! I'll miss them, too. They were the kindest, most caring and efficient group of people that you would ever hope to have care for you. They even gave me a graduation certificate that I will treasure always.

No one said so, but they gave me the feeling that I had graduated with honors. I felt so blessed that it's hard to put into words. So, with certificate in hand, I simply hugged everyone plus all the people in the waiting room that I had come to know as friends and floated out, "glowing," renewed and blessed out of my socks.

"Where, O death,

Is your victory?

Where, O death,

Is thy sting?"

1Corinthians 12:55

"A heart at peace gives

Life to the body."

Proverbs 14:30

Radiation treatments were painless and over quickly, probably twenty minutes each time after I was correctly situated under the radiation arm. Nothing touched my skin except the beams of "light." The machine made some strange noises as it moved around to the different "zapping" areas and before I knew it, I would be told, "That's it for today. See you tomorrow."

In March 2007, after a C-scan, the Lung Specialist dismissed me with his blessings. The scar on my lung showed no change, either from cancer or damage from the radiation treatments. There is always a danger with radiation that some damage will be done to adjoining tissue to those being radiated.

I was so pleased when he pronounced me too healthy for him to treat at this time.

In April 2007, I had follow-up tests with the Oncology Group and a week later I went to see the Oncologist for the test results. He came in with a big smile on his face and began to tell me how happy he was to see me doing so well. Remember he had told me in January that my tumor was gone, so this wasn't a surprise.

After talking with me for a few more minutes he said, "You know that I was not pleased when you refused to have Chemotherapy, but I was wrong and you were right."

This was a surprise that I didn't expect, but how refreshing to hear a doctor who would admit that he was wrong. But I assured him that it wasn't a decision that I had made without much prayer and that God had given me a peace to proceed without Chemotherapy.

The doctor then said, "Well, you can't go wrong heeding His directions. You heard directly from the big boss."

His final word as he walked out the door was, "Congratulations!"

I'm truly amazed how God's hand moves invisibly, yet invincibly, to bring His sovereign plan to completion, no matter how tragic things seem to us at the time. Our God is a God of surprises and He always wins. What great comfort that brings!

There will be follow up tests and I will remain on the oral medication for now. Just where all this ends, no one but God knows and that, too, is as it should be, for God always does things right! His way is always the best way, even if to us, it seems to be wrong. Plus, His timing is perfect!

You can be sure that He will always give you what you need at the appropriate time, for God gives the very best to those who leave the choices and timing up to Him. If you ask God for one thing and receive another… simply walk in faith and trust Him for the outcome!

I'm walking in that faith and I have a new "glow" which I tell everyone is not from radiation therapy but from prayer therapy. The very best therapy of all therapies is *prayer therapy* and I am visible proof of that. I feel so covered with prayers that they have become a lifeline to hold close to my heart, not just for now, but always.

I feel completely safe knowing that God is always in control and that when He decides He is ready for me to join Him, I am ready for the trip so covered with prayers that the trip would simply be a glorious new adventure …and I love adventure.

So, pray on!

A motto to live by:

Do all the good you can. By all the means you can. In all the ways you can. In all the places you can. At all the times you can. To all the people you can. As long as ever you can.

John Wesley

Cancer is a disease of the mind, body, and spirit. A proactive and positive attitude will help the cancer warrior be a survivor. Anger, unforgiveness, and bitterness all put the body into a stressful and acidic environment. Learn to have a loving and forgiving spirit.

I do not want it said of me and cancer that I have fought it for all these many years. It is true that cancer and I have traveled together at times, but in between times I haven't given it any power over my thoughts. God's "It's OK" fills my thoughts and I am too content to waste my energy fighting a defeated foe. It's that "win-win" situation that I'm enjoying that comforts me.

Learn to relax and enjoy life.

"By Grace alone, through Faith alone,

in Christ alone,

for the glory of God alone.

For from Him and through Him

and to Him are all things.

To Him be the glory forever!

Amen!"

Romans 11:36

"So will it be with the resurrection
of the dead.
The body that is sown is perishable,
it is raised imperishable;
it is sown in dishonor,
it is raised in glory;
it is sown in weakness,
it is raised in power;
it is sown a natural body,
it is raised as a spiritual body.
If there is a natural body,
there is also a spiritual body."

1 Corinthians 15:42-44

"There is both beauty and pain in
this 'shadow world'
we live in.
There will be only beauty
without pain
in the glorious Heaven to come.
Blessed are you who weep now,
for you will laugh.
Rejoice in that day and leap with joy,
because
great is your reward in Heaven."

Luke 6:21-23

Consider this as another end of another beginning!

(And life still goes on!)

Because life is still going on…

A thought to remember about our
Christian walk through this life:

"We are not human beings going through
a temporary spiritual experience.

We are spiritual beings going through
a temporary human experience."

Note:

Where I first heard this wonderful thought on life as a Christian was from my favorite pastor, Paul Owens. Paul has taught me so much more about the sovereignty of God and His truly amazing grace than I ever knew before. Paul's leadership, based on his firm belief in the sovereignty of a loving, all powerful God, has helped me grow and mature as a child of this truly amazing God we serve. I am blessed to consider Paul and his wife, Rhoda, as my "children" and they honored me by calling me their "mother-in-love."

I constantly thank God for putting them and all my Christian friends in my life. It is a heartfelt blessing that I cannot find words to adequately express. Just know that it has been and continues to be a great joy. Sharing life with those who know and love Christ as you do is a wonderful experience!

Chapter 8
Poems from My Heart

I have been told that you can only hear poetry with your heart, so I ask you to open your hearts to the following poems that have touched my heart. Some that God spoke to me and I hope that what I heard will be what you hear. There are poems that He spoke to other listening hearts and my prayer is that you will also hear what God wanted them to hear.

I'll begin with a poem written by my nephew, Mark. Mark is quite an accomplished poet, although he probably would frown on my saying so. In his poem, "A Poet's Eye," he says, "Poetry allows us to express in a uniquely artistic way, what we might otherwise be unwilling or unable to say." I find that to be very true, sometimes we are unable to give oral expression to our deepest and sometimes our most loving and caring thoughts. When they find expression through the poems that God writes on our hearts, then we are able to share what we otherwise could not.

Mark is a very special man in many ways and his walk with the Lord has included a very difficult path, which he has endured with an acceptance that only comes with walking closely with God. As a young man just out of college and beginning to work in his chosen field of architecture, he was diagnosed with myotonic dystrophy, a form of muscular dystrophy.

Soon, he was not able to hold drawing instruments, so he went back to college to get a degree that would fit his disability.

His condition has worsened to the point that he falls often, without being able to get himself up, and he has limited upper arm strength… but at 47 years of age, he still lives alone, drives to work, and plans to be independent as long as possible.

I have never heard the first “poor me” come out of his mouth. He is a truly wonderful and inspiring man.

As you read these poems that follow, see them with the eyes of your heart. Let your heart be open to the music that the poet heard and has written with the hope that you hear the music, too.

A Poet's Eye

It's not that I consider myself an authority,
but this is what I consider poets and poetry to be.
It might make the point easier to see,
if I express it in the form of poetry.
Poetry allows us to express in a uniquely artistic way,
what we might otherwise be unwilling or unable to say.
One can write poetry for the art of poetry's sake,
or to escape the trials of life which seem at times too hard to take.
One reason why poetry is important to us all,
is that it can encourage us to try again when we fall.
Poetry can be serious in an attempt to set wrongs right,
or, to appreciate beauty such as the effortless grace of an eagle in flight.
There are no rules as some would dictate,
conformity would miss the point that poetry can uniquely make.
A free mind unencumbered by rules,
allow poets to draw from deeper pools.
Imagination and words are the tools of a poet's trade,
it is with these that the foundation of poetry is laid.
Poets see things in a different way,
as different from most as night and day.
Anything is possible in the poet's eye,
natural laws and physics do not necessarily apply.
A poet sees God painting with clouds on a canvas of blue sky,
cats that talk, fish that walk and pigs that really do fly.
These are just some of the things that a poet makes us see,
and although we know better, it seems at times it just might be.
Poets don't worry too much about such details,
their only concern is with provoking thought and blazing new trails.
Poetry paints a picture of something imagined or real,
a picture you can see in your mind but more importantly feel.
It isn't necessarily a structured poem or Shakespearean play,
poetry is simply expressing yourself in an imaginative way.
A poem can be written in any form or style you wish to choose.
Poetry written to please yourself really can't lose.

Mark Daniel Harrison

Don't Quit!

When things go wrong, as they sometimes will.
When the road you're trudging seems all up hill,
when the funds are low and the debts are high,
and you want to smile but you have to sigh.
When care is pressing you down a bit,
rest if you must…but don't you quit!

Life is queer with its twists and turns,
as everyone of us sometimes learns.
And many a failure turns about
when he would have won had he stuck it out.
Don't give up though the pace seems slow.
You might succeed…with another blow!

Often the goal is nearer than
it seems to a faint and faltering man.
Often the struggler has given up
when he might have captured the victor's cup.
And he learned too late, when the night slipped down
how close he was…to the golden crown!

Success is failure turned inside out;
the silver tint of the clouds of doubt.
And you never can tell how close you are,
it may be near when it seems afar.
So stick to the fight when you're hardest hit.
It's when things seem worst…that you mustn't quit!

Author Unknown

Words from God about perseverance:

"However, I consider my life worth nothing to me, if only I may finish the race and complete the task the Lord Jesus Christ has given me…the task of testifying to the gospel of God's grace."

Acts 20:24

"However,
"I have fought the good fight, I have finished the race, I have kept the faith."

2 Timothy 4:7

"Therefore, since we are surrounded by such a great cloud of witnesses, let us throw off everything that hinders and the sin that so easily entangles, and let us run with perseverance the race marked out for us."

Hebrews 12:1

TALL ON MY KNEES

Lord,
why am I here,
down on my knees?
I cry many a bitter tear,
struggling to stand up right.
Yet,
here I am,
weak and alone.
Surrounded by despair…
what am I to learn?
Is it that from here,
small on my knees,
there is nothing to do,
but look up,
into Your loving face?
Yes! Now, I know.
I'm here,
just where You want me to be.
In Your arms,
Your power resting on me.
I'm here where I belong,
knowing Your Grace is sufficient.
For only here am I strong:
boasting of my weaknesses,
tall on my knees.

However,
"But He said to me, 'My Grace is sufficient for you, for my power is made perfect in weakness.'
Therefore I will boast all the more gladly about my weaknesses,
so that Christ's power may rest on me.
That is why, for Christ's sake,
I delight in weaknesses,
in insults, in hardships,
in persecutions, in difficulties.
For when I am weak, then I am strong."

11 Corinthians 12:9-10

THE RIVER

All of life, its happiness and sorrows;
the journey we make, everything we experience
becomes a part of us.
We are the sum of all those who touch our lives.
(Parents, siblings, teachers, friends, mates and children)
Those we love, those who love us;
not always with understanding.
But knowing that we can love completely,
without understanding completely.
Eventually all things merge into one;
and love is the river that runs through it.
Flowing in and out,
sometimes shallow, barely there,
other times very deep and serene.
Occasionally raging,
spilling out of its banks, uncontrolled and flooding.
Sweeping us away with its power.
Tearing apart, then gently pulling together again.
But always there, always…flowing onward.
Life without love is an empty riverbed,
an existence…but without meaning.
God is Love.
He must be the one who most touches our lives,
for only He loves completely with complete understanding.
His river never runs dry.
I'm blessed by love, haunted by love, saved by love
…flowing ever onward.

However,
“There is a river
whose streams make glad
the city of God,
the holy place
where
the Most High dwells.”

Psalm 46:4

About the river of life, a very wise man once said, “You can never step in the same river twice.” Each day is a new day, a new beginning and His river that is flowing onward is ever fresh and ever new.

THE SECRET PLACE

There is a special place, one so secret,
it is only known to you and God.
A haven of safety and peace;
A harbor free from trouble and strife,
In which your heart can rest.
A home where your spirit, untroubled,
can quietly abide.
Becoming a shelter of love for a soul…
"that dwelleth in the secret place
of the Most High"…
When doubts and fear assail you,
And your peace is gone,
You have stepped out from your
secret place.
Quickly turn your heart toward home.
Hasten to return to that shelter of love.
Creep back into that safe haven of peace,
your secret place;
that harbor known only to you and God.
To … "*abide under the shadow of the Almighty."*

"He that dwelleth in the secret place
of the Most High,
Shall abide under the
Shadow of the Almighty."

Psalm 91:1

A WALL BUILDER

As the Master Architect
God's miracles are not always
the work of a moment;
but are often walls made of bricks.
Sometimes bricks of failure,
formed in a world of sin,
cemented with mortar of remorse.
Walls that crumble against the slightest
push of evil,
having to be rebuilt again and again.
As with Peter,
who thought his was a mighty wall,
yet he failed
God three times,
let me learn through my failures.
In this world that violates God's law,
profanes His Holy Name;
teach me to faithfully stand in the gap.
Rebuilding walls of moral decay
with bricks of faith.
Bricks baked in the kiln of His Grace;
cemented with His Love.
Help me be a steadfast wall builder,
standing in the gap,
following the Master Architect's plan,
rebuilding the wall
one brick of faith at a time.

However,
"I looked for a man among them
who would build up the wall
and stand before me
in the gap on behalf of the land
so I would not have to
destroy it, but found none."

Ezekiel 22:30

PAID IN FULL

I have a statement that says my account is closed,
my debt paid in full.
It is found in God's word,
the Holy Bible.
Therein is declared the good news
of God's unfailing love for me.
A love so great,
He sent His only Son to die for me.
God took all my sin debts,
nailed them with His Son
to Calvary's Cross.
The Sinless there to die for every sin.
Then in glorious resurrection,
the Son ascended to the Father,
with a promise to return for me.
Sitting there at the right hand
of the Father,
seeing every mistake I'll ever make,
knowing them all beforehand,
He lovingly intercedes for me.
Holding my bills clutched in
His nail-scarred hands,
He stamps them with His own
precious blood.
Then, with a smile, gives them to the Father,
marked…
"ACCOUNT CLOSED/PAID IN FULL"

"For God so loved the world that
He gave His one and only Son,
that whoever believes in Him
shall not perish but
have eternal life."

John 3:16

BORN TO FLY

Here am I, a lowly creature bound to a slow
spinning orb we call earth; looking into the sky,
watching the larks and eagles soar.
And wingless though I may be,
wishing I, too, could fly.
Dreaming of riding the winds,
my spirit joyfully sailing over and under sunlit clouds.
Sweeping through endless time and space.
Just me…
Surrounded by nothing of the human race.
Just me…
Free and floating in the pristine air.
Rising higher and higher without a single care;
until my soul, timidly felt
the touch of God's reaching hand.
Then with heart filled with wonder, I realize…
He was there waiting for me to find,
that my dream was part of what He long ago planned.
He wanted me to discover my "butterfly wings,"
to make my metamorphosis complete.
Then in a voice so gentle and sweet,
I heard words of such joy that my heart still sings.
He said, "My child, you were born to fly;
I was just waiting for you to try."

"…I will redeem you with an out-stretched arm and with mighty acts of judgment."

Exodus 6:6

I AM BEAUTIFUL, I AM LOVED, I AM FREE TO SOAR!
or
METAMORPHOSIS BY GRACE

Thinking of my past, I found myself trapped
in a cocoon of despair, rejection, self-pity.
Feeling unloved, unworthy, hiding in the darkness,
alone and sad; wondering how God could possibly
love a worm like me.
Then I heard His voice softly whisper,
"My child, there is nothing you could do
that could make me love you any more than I do now
and certainly nothing that you could ever do
will make Me love you less.
You are truly forgiven;
I remember your past no more."
Suddenly…My heart leaping, I knew it was only me
that saw the lowly caterpillar.
God had always seen the beautiful butterfly.
As I realized this,
He gently lifted me up out of my earthbound cocoon,
to soar on gossamer wings of glistening joy,
a beautiful new creature, reborn, through His Grace.
A gift born of God's great love through His Son,
unearned, unconditional, eternal and absolutely free.
Will I ever be a caterpillar again?
No, never! The caterpillar was crucified with Christ.
Now, I'm forever a brilliant butterfly of paradise!
I am beautiful, I am loved, I am free to soar!

"What use the glad wings
of a butterfly,
if it is earthbound with
thoughts of its
contemptible past?"

Unknown

THE VOICE DIVINE

God speaks to us in many ways,
His voice is everywhere.
Wind whistling in the trees,
the laughter of children playing without a care.
The cheerful chirping of a bird;
all these beautiful sounds of nature,
seem like prayers when heard.
The music of His voice, so wonderfully powerful;
rolling, crashing thunder can't compete.
Yet, too, a tiny whisper, so exquisitely tender;
we hear it as we sleep.
Sounds of love, beautiful, powerful, tender and sweet,
to soothe heart and mind.
Echoing from Heaven above comes the voice of God,
…the voice divine.

*"Whether you turn to the right or
to the left, your ears will hear
a voice behind you saying,
"This is the way; walk in it."*

Isaiah 30:21

A PROMISE: BRUISED NOT BROKEN

There are times when everything seems out of control, when it
seems even God is silent.
Yet, we know, nothing is out of God's control.
He is not still.
Be faithful,
we are often ushered into His presence
on wings of storms.
God allows Satan to sift us,
then blows away our chaff.
Letting us sink to the lowest in order to move upward
toward His highest.
Emptying us of worldliness
before filling us with Godliness.
God waits on those who are humble, hungry, inadequate, hoping
only in Him.
What an amazing victory in the surrender
of our will;
when we move from our brokenness into
His wholeness;
never to be broken again.
Bruised, maybe…battered, maybe,
but never again broken!

"A bruised reed He will not break."

Isaiah 42:3

EYES OF THE HEART

With the eyes of your heart
see the beauty that surrounds you.
God's Love manifested in His handiwork;
glorious sunrises, beautiful sunsets,
days of joyous splendor,
nights soft as silk.
Magnificent mountains regal with caps of snow,
serene lakes endlessly reflecting azure skies,
laughing children innocently at play;
beauty in sparkling youth, serenity in golden age.

With the eyes of your heart
look, too, at those around you.
See their suffering, the hurts life has inflicted,
their hearts bleeding, crying out in pain;
wanting someone to care.
Reach out, give them the healing balm of your sharing.
Heed the needs of the poor and downtrodden,
fill their emptiness with His love.
Give from the bounty of joy that bubbles up within you.

With the eyes of your heart
See God in everything,
both the good and the bad.
For in His infinite wisdom, He has allowed it.
He is Sovereign. He is in complete control.
From Him all things flow and with Him all things are possible.

So, with the eyes of your heart look at all, with His Love.
Be filled with great joy, and know that in His Kingdom, truly
…all is well

"I pray also that the eyes of your heart
may be enlightened in order
that you may know the hope
to which He has called you,
the riches of His glorious inheritance
in the saints, and His incomparably
great power for us who believe.

Ephesians 1:18 & 19

QUAKES

As I walked down life's weary path,
failure, rejection and abject poverty of spirit
my only companions;
I felt a violent tremor, a force buffeting
me on all sides.
The whole earth shook…or did it?
Was the earthquake only in my soul?
Could this act of God be just for me:
to shake me out of my self-pity?
Just then, magically I felt my soul being lifted.
Only, this was not a magic carpet ride…
it was angels' wings,
taking me from the pit of despair, lifting me to
soar higher and higher.
Unbelieving, drawn to look down again,
I found myself falling back into the abyss of
doubt and fear;
suffering an aftershock, new tremors of my soul.
But there they were, those angelic beings
following me down,
to softly and tenderly catch me up again.
Then, still unbelieving,
I looked once more into that bottomless chasm…
Oh, no! Another aftershock. Help me; I'm falling!
Unbelievably rescued…caught midair,
to be cradled securely and lifted up yet again.
This time, elevated above all doubt, all fear,
lifted by the power of God's Love…
'the wind beneath the angels' wings,'
to be swept into His Presence.
His Amazing Grace
forever quieting the quakes of my soul.

*"However,
I bore you on eagles' wings and
brought you to Myself."*

Exodus 19:4

(To me, these eagles' wings are the angels' wings described in Quakes!)

SING IN YOUR PAIN

Earth-bound spirits can never soar,
so be heavenly minded.
Every blessing, every joy sent by God
loosens a strand that binds you to earth.
Broken hearts can mend,
spirits regain strength, find joy not dreamed of before.
With God's love in your heart,
the beauty of each day will live on long after
pain and sorrow have passed.
So, with heaven-bound spirit soaring,
sing in your pain.
Across the bleakest of days
shines the light of God's love
Live with a joyful heart, no running from the past.
No looking back except to learn.
God is your Physician,
The Great Healer of body and soul.
His promise is, "Behold, I make all things new."
We are new every morning.
So…in spite of present sorrow,
send a song of thanksgiving floating heavenward,
joyfully singing in your pain.

"But I will sing of Your power,
Yes I will sing aloud of Your mercy in the morning.
For You have been my defense
and refuge in the day of my trouble."

Psalm 59:16

LOVE…GOD'S FAVORITE REMEDY

When disappointment overtakes us,
one note of joy thrills through the pain…
Love!.
For brave hearts with wounded spirits,
there is one solace through which we gain…
Love!
What are these strong wings for weak souls,
comfort for the broken heart?
Love!
What can turn evil into good,
move mountains, make rivers part?
Love!
What always stands by you through thick and thin,
turns defeats into victories that we win?
Love!
God created Love,
gives Love to us in abundance, absolutely free.
How do we know?
Simple, it was Love and Love alone
that held Jesus to the tree.
God's Love is healing, the remedy, the "Balm of Gilead,"
the "Great Physician's" eternal cure for you and me.

"Your love, O God, reaches to the heavens,
Your faithfulness to the skies."

Psalm 36:5

THE SHADOW

"Yea, though I walk through the valley of the shadow of death..." Psalm 23:4

Yes, death is just a shadow, a shadow in
the shape of a Cross; reflected by the Son's light.
A light of magnificent love…
shining at the end of the valley, leading us
through life and "death."
Not covered with darkness but shielded by Grace.
Life, too, is but a shadow, a shadow in the
shape of a single man; hands out-stretched.
A brilliant light from heaven, shining
through the nail scarred hands…
spot-lighting each of the faithful with
rays of forgiveness.
On the Cross, bearing all our pain,
His death. a sacrificial gift.
There is no love greater than this.
There is nothing in life or death not covered
by the shadow of Christ and His cross.
His amazing Grace is both light and shadow.
A light of everlasting love…
His Love encompasses all.
A shadow of sinless death…
His surrogate death was for every sin,
our debt paid in full.
His resurrection ensures eternal life.
No longer shadow…only Holy Light.

WORTH THE WAIT

When every day is filled
with only sadness and strife;
you begin to wonder,
isn't there more than this to life.
Be calm, seek not knowledge of the future;
what's written on every page.
Begin each day with love and laughter;
just face the storms as they rage.
Know sorrow may endure
for the long dark night.
But peace and joy comes with the morning light.
So, possess your soul in patience and rejoice.
Waiting of the Lord
is always the best choice.
For in the waiting you will find…
God is too good to be unkind.

*"but those who hope in the Lord
will renew their strength.
They will soar on wings like eagles,
They will run and not grow weary,
They will walk and not be faint."*

Isaiah 40:31

GOD'S GARDEN

We live in a world of beauty, a treasure
just waiting to be shared.
As you pass through God's Garden,
stop, take time to listen with your heart
to the music of a babbling brook,
cascading merrily over stones, laughing,
forever on its way.
Hear the trilling of a cheerful bird,
flying on a lazy breeze, happy with its lot.
Hark to the gentle sigh of wind in the swaying trees,
singing love songs to every listening ear.
All these melodies are poetry
from the very heart of God.

Look at the beautiful flowers strewn along your path,
nodding happily, vivid in the glorious sunny day.
Just as they reflect their joy
in the raindrops softly falling,
washing their petals with loving care.
See the brilliant rainbow, a radiant signal;
the raging storm has passed.
Magnificent sunrise, splendid sunset,
soft glow of moonrise, the twinkling of distant stars;
all mirror the beauty of God's Creation.
Filling both eye and heart with symbols of
His Everlasting Love.

Yes, there is beauty everywhere,
surrounding our days and nights;
giving endless joy to those who seek it.
Look for this beauty, this joy, until it becomes
a living part of your very soul.
When your heart breaks with the joy of holding this treasure close;
give it back to the world in the form of a smile,
a loving word, a kind and thoughtful act…
or a prayer of thanksgiving.
Remembering always,
there are forever the gleams of "Son-Light" to bring
His beauty and joy into the garden of your soul.

*"You will be a well-watered garden,
like a spring whose waters never fail."*

Isaiah 58:11

JUST FOR YOU

(three poems dedicated to the most wonderful gift I ever received,
a gift directly from God: my son
...David Manon Morgan, born Christmas day 1959)

From the first time your tiny little fist
uncurled, to encircle one of my fingers,
I knew we had begun a journey;
just you and I.
A wonderful journey that would be
like no other experience,
either of us
would share with another;
just you and I.
A miraculous journey of love that I
till then, never knew existed.
A growing through trial and error,
error mostly mine, but always together;
just you and I.
For when your precious little hand
first reached to touch mine,
it wasn't only my finger you took.
You reached in and captured my heart.
Beginning a journey into forever;
just you and I.

Evelyne Morgan McCollum

A PRAYER FOR FORGIVENESS

Forgive me for not telling you as you first kicked
in my womb,
for waiting until you had almost grown
to let you know always, just how much God loves you.
It was your right, you should have known.
It was my mistake not to realize
how much even then you needed to know
that my love for you would always be there,
to grow and grow.
But, that God's love was even greater than mine.
And here is how you can know that;
because from the beginning, God couldn't love you more
and would never love you less than now.
To Him, you are completely worthy just as you are.
Your worth to Him, nothing can ever mar.
He isn't waiting for you to change to love you.
He loves you just as you are.
Please realize, my son,
God will forgive you anything you ask Him to.
He wants nothing more than that you love Him,
as much as He loves you.
God blessed me beyond measure,
when He gave you to me to love.
But from the very start I always knew,
you really belonged to your Father above.
I ask you to remember it's never too late
to give Him your heart.
He'll lift you up, hold you in His arms,
as He gives you a brand new start.
I loved you from the start,
I love you now,
But tomorrow I'll love you even more still.
God loved you from the start,
He loves you now,
and always will!

Your Mom, Evelyne Morgan McCollum

MATERNAL MUSE ON A MALE CHILD GROWN

Tears and laughter, frustration and joy,
you brought all this into my life.
From the beginning, joy;
Growing to love you more each day.
Watching your wonder at things around you;
my wonder, at how fast you learned and grew.
Laughing with you when happy times
made each day golden.
Crying with you when you hurt;
those times when life was full of pain.
Frustration when you went your way,
(as was your right) but not the path I chose.
But always, love. No need to earn it;
couldn't stop it if you tried.
You are a miracle, God's love gift to me.
A very special treasure…His own little lamb.
I love you …did from day one;
not knowing then how much that love would grow.
I will love you forever…
with a love too awesome not to share.
So, I give you back to God, every day in my prayers,
for I can have no greater joy,
than that my child walk in His truth.
Yours is the future. You are free to be everything
God has planned you to be.
Know that my love is surpassed only by His,
and that we both will love you eternally!

NEW BEGINNINGS IN THE NEW YEAR
(any year)

One of the best things we can do in our lives is this:

Begin again.
Begin to see yourself
as you were when you were the happiest
and strongest you've ever been.

Begin to remember
what worked for you and what worked against you,
and try to capture the magic again.

Begin to remember
how natural it was when you were a child,
to live a lifetime each day.

Begin to forget
the baggage you have carried with you for years.
The problems that don't matter anymore, the tears that cried themselves away, and the worries that are going to wash away on the shore of tomorrow's

NEW BEGINNINGS.

Tomorrow tells us it will be here every new day
of our lives; and if we will be wise, we will turn away from the problems of the past and give the future and ourselves a chance to become the best of friends.

Sometimes all it takes is a wish in the heart
to let yourself…simply Begin again.

Author known only by God

HOLE OR WHOLE?

My days are sad; my nights are long,
I am not happy, what is wrong?
There is no lack of "things," I have all that I need;
but having doesn't bring joy, there's a hunger "having" does not feed.
My heart cries out in loneliness and fear;
I pray, "Who will help me, who will hear?
Lord, why do I feel so empty, why am I so cold?"
His answer came back, "Because, in your heart there is a gaping hole,
an emptiness that all your things can never fill.
It's Me you need, for nothing else your fears will still.
Die to the world and in Me, a new life you'll gain.
For My love and only My love can take away the pain.
You're My Chosen one;
you are holy and dearly loved by Me.
My child, you must come to see,
that without Me your heart will always have a hole,
accept Me, then your life and your heart will be whole.
You can win or lose,
hole or whole, which do you choose?"

"I will give you a new heart and put a new spirit in you; I will remove from you your heart of stone and give you a heart of flesh."

Ezekiel 36:26

MARKED AND SEALED

Holy Spirit, speak to me,
be the faith I cannot see.
Tell me how to live this day…
do I rest, do I pray?
Fill me with Your awesome power,
and with Thy peace fill this hour.

Holy spirit, be with me,
help me more like Thee to be.
Help me a better life to live,
as all to Thee I freely give.
For me, with the Father intercede,
make my will to His will agreed.

Holy Spirit, fill me up,
let me drink from God's cup.
Help me die to self,
so that only God's love is left.
Help me more like Christ to be,
until His precious face I see!

However,
"And you also were included in
Christ when you heard the truth,
the gospel of your salvation.
Having believed, you were marked
in Him with a seal,
the promised Holy Spirit,
who is a deposit guaranteeing
our inheritance until the
redemption of those who were
God's possessions…
to the praise of His Glory."

Ephesians 1:13 & 14

SONG IN THE NIGHT

God's Love is a song
in the darkness of my despair.
His song of Love
lifts my worldly care.
The music fills my soul,
healing my broken heart,
making it whole.
The melody still resounding
loud and clear.
Each note proclaiming
God is always near.
The angels still singing
of wrongs made right.
Yes, His Love comes softly
as a song in the night.

Chorus:

Melody, oh so sweet,
over and over to repeat;
God is Love.
God is Love.
Yes, His Love is a song,
a song in the night.

FOUR POEMS BY A FRIEND

LITTLE LIGHTENING BUG

Compared to the stars by night
gleaming and shining, so bright.
Steadfast in their courses, fly
lifted up so lofty, high.

I'm a little lightening bug
captured in a bottle, jug.
In erratic patterns, fly
flicker briefly, then I die.

This the joy that fuels my flight
as I praise with all my might
that Your Awesome Love for me
will last of Eternity.

LORD OF ALL

Lord of all my ugliness
and Lord of all my pride.
Lord of all my wickedness,
Your Blood to me applied.

Lord of all my wretchedness
and now my Holy Guide.
Lord of all my righteousness
You walk close
by my side.

Lord of all my living days
all that I am You see.
Lord of all with loving gaze,
this truth that sets me free.

STORMS OF LIFE

Centered in the storms of life,
surrounded by sin and strife,
lost amid the raging winds,
are choices where nobody wins.

Is there hope for tomorrow,
from this life's pain and sorrow?
Do we know where we're going?
Have we learned what You're showing?

When I trust in Your embrace,
to endure the storms I face,
I will know sufficient Grace.
Then storms will pass without a trace.

THE ESSENCE OF GRACE

Forgiven and made brand new
walking hand in hand with You
and looking upon Your face
This is the essence of Grace.

My heart has been befriended
my mind has been defended.
I'm strengthened to run this race.
This is the essence of Grace.

Blessing on blessing poured out
knowing You I want to shout.
Chosen regardless of 'case.'
This is the essence of Grace.

Louise D. Megargee

The following three poems were written by a 15 year old young girl. She is the granddaughter of Louise Megargee. I have included them because I am blown away by the insight of such a young person, who is wise beyond her years.. May she continue to share her insight through poetry as she grows into a mature and even wiser young woman.

LIFE

Everyone is good enough.
Everyone is right.
Everyone deserves a home,
and a warm bed at night.

Everybody needs a friend.
Everyone needs their space.
All people are equal,
so why is there a human race?

Maybe our only problem is…
That some refuse to see…
not everyone else is the trouble.
The trouble is you and me.

So if we work together…
as a team, you and me…
May be we can rebuild our world
and make all our dreams come true.

BELIEVE IN YOURSELF

Set your standards high,
you deserve the best.
Try for what you want,
and never settle for less.

Believe in yourself,
no matter what you choose.
Keep a winning attitude,
and you can never lose.

Think about your destination,
but don't worry if you stray.
Because the most important thing
is what you learn along the way.

Take all that you've become
to be all that you can.
Soar above the clouds
and let your dreams set you free.

I CAN WALK ON WATER

I can walk on water
and if I want to I can fly.
I'll sit upon the sun
and watch the world go by.
I am who I want to be,
I hold onto life with a grip.
I think about everything,
the future and the past.
My body is made from the earth,
my soul is made from the sky.
My life is part of nature's gift.
I taste the ocean when I cry.
My tears will live forever,
they will never die.
Maybe as the wind or grass,
but I promise you they will last.
I am eternity,
I will never fade.
I am the stuff
by which you were made.
I can walk on water
and if I want to I can fly.
I can do whatever,
all I have to do is try.

Stacey D. Megargee

A poem set to music

WAIT FOR THE LORD

Wait for the Lord in the days of sunshine.
Wait for the Lord in the nights of shadows.
He will find you in your darkest hour
And bring you even closer through His Son!

Wait, yes, wait for the Lord.

Be strong, take heart and trust in Him!
And then in His own time,
He will bless you again.
Wait for the Lord, Your God!

Lyrics by: Evelyne McCollum
Music by: Teresa Caudle**

"Wait for the Lord;
be strong and take heart
and wait for the Lord."

Psalm 27:14

** Teresa Caudle is Evelyne's niece and a very accomplished vocalist, plus she has the ability to hear music in a poem and put that music on paper. God gifted her with many talents, which she uses to share her faith with many people. Teresa is a very devout Christian and has raised two wonderful children who also love the Lord with all their hearts.

Teresa is also a cancer survivor. She has had a double mastectomy with reconstruction surgery. During her ordeal she requested prayers that she would walk through it in a manner that would glorify God. She did that with a great dignity. There was a complication when as a result of surgery she lost her voice, not just her singing voice but also her speaking one. She considered this much more tragic than the cancer. But praise God, He did return her voice and it is even better than before.

Later, she was given medical opinions that she is now cancer free and should remain so for at least 10 years. She and I both praise the Lord for His faithfulness.

God is good all the time!

All the time God is good!

Evelyne McCollum
Teresa Caudle

WAIT FOR THE LORD
(Psalm 27:14)

In conclusion, I must say that there are many more people that have walked this walk with me. Some very good friends that have been blessed with remission and some that God has taken home to be with Him.

Each of these dear ladies have their own story of how cancer impacted their lives and the lives of those they loved - often a much more dramatic story than the one written here.

Let me repeat something I mentioned earlier: Cancer is a disease of the mind, body, and spirit. A devout faith in the Sovereign Lord of the universe along with a proactive and positive spirit will help the cancer warrior to be a survivor.

Anger, unforgiveness and bitterness put the body into a stressful and acidic environment. Learn to have a loving and forgiving spirit. Learn to relax and enjoy life. And never forget that God is in control of all things and that includes cancer.

Faith sees the invisible,
believes the incredible,
and
receives the seemly impossible.

Again, I ask you to always remember the things that cancer cannot do:

Cancer is so limited…
It cannot cripple
LOVE
It cannot shatter
HOPE
It cannot corrode
FAITH
It cannot destroy
PEACE
It cannot kill
FRIENDSHIP
It cannot suppress
MEMORIES
It cannot silence
COURAGE
It cannot invade the
SOUL
It cannot steal
ETERNAL LIFE
It cannot conquer the
SPIRIT

Author Unknown

I want to leave you with my favorite Bible verse. This verse strengthens me to walk calmly through any situation that I find myself in. I hope it calms your spirit, too.

"I have told you these things, so that in Me you may have peace. In this world you will have troubles. But take heart! I have overcome the world." John 16:33

My prayer for everyone who reads this book is that it will be an inspiration of help and truly bless all that walk the cancer road or have a loved one that trods this uneasy path.

This book is meant in its entirety to simply and completely honor God as the "Great Physician" and to glorify Him in every way.

Life still goes on for now!

In His love, Evelyne McCollum

To Order Copies of

The Gift of Time

by Evelyne J. McCollum

ISBN 1-59879-700-X

Order Online at:

www.LifeVestBooks.com

By Phone Toll Free at:

1-877-843-1007

LifeVest PUBLISHING, INC.